Words of Light and Midnight
Poems from a Pagan Priest

P. B. Owl

a BlackWyrm book
Louisville, Kentucky

WORDS OF LIGHT AND MIDNIGHT

Copyright ©2013 by BlackWyrm Publishing

All rights reserved, including the right to reproduce this book, or portion thereof, in any form. Written permission must be secured from the publisher to use or reproduce any part of this book, except for brief quotations in critical reviews or articles.

A BlackWyrm Book
BlackWyrm Publishing
10307 Chimney Ridge Ct, Louisville, KY 40299

Printed in the United States of America.

ISBN: 978-1-61318-154-6

Cover Design: P. B. Owl
Cover Photography: Lisa Marcum (Minerva of WynDragon Family)
Author Photography: Wayne "Thag" Walls

First edition: September 2013

Dedicated to:

Mau du' Owlwyn, Priestess and partner.

Lady Kelshei and other assorted Ladies in sundry Circles.

The WynDragon Family.

Black Wyrm Publications, for giving me this opportunity.

Thag Jenkins, the Littlest Gravel Angel.

Introduction

This is a collected work of poetry. You can read it with no previous conceptions or similar experiences to the author's, just as people have read poetry for thousands of years. At least it is my hope that the mystery, imagery, color, and magic of these pieces can stand on their own in the way that poetry sometimes does, and that the best of poetry always does.

If you want to read this book as a window into a different culture or point of view, you can do that, too. I am a Wiccan Priest and Elder, and these works were written from that point of view, many of them to meet the specific needs of my church, congregation, and community. If you have no previous experience with Wicca or any other forms of modern Paganism, then let me briefly state that Paganism in general and Wicca as it's best known form are nature based, polytheistic or pantheistic faiths with an emphasis on personal responsibility and the ability of all people to remake the world into a better place, starting with one person at a time, themselves. For the past 20 years they have been the fastest growing forms of worship in North America. A lot of these pieces were written in rhyme or rhythm in part due to the traditional use of these elements in Wiccan liturgy and ceremonial work. To quote an extended version of our most famous piece of liturgy, the Wiccan Rede, "To bind the spell well every time, let the spell be spoken in rhyme" (THE WICCAN REDE, Mark Ventimiglia, p.16).

If you are Pagan or Wiccan, many of the pieces here will be familiar in form. I have included some specific suggestions on how some of these types of poems can be used by the individual or a group in religious practice. I have also arranged them in a rough sort of order as to how they are experienced both in religious practice and then in personal experience. Many of these pieces are from a masculine viewpoint, again, I am male and serve as a priest so it colors my poetic work as well as my life's work. Please feel free to take inspiration from this book and adapt these pieces for your own ritual work (just please don't change a word or two and republish, this makes old priests sad).

Some of these pieces have been previously published in a variety of Pagan magazines and periodicals, but as is standard practice in our community, republication rights remain with the author.

I have lit the Candle, I have rung the Bell. It is up to you to open the Book.

Blessed Be,

P. B. Owl

Table of Contents

Invocations
A Circle Song 2
Elemental Chant 3
The Horned Lord at High
    Spring 4
Summer Lord 5
Sing the Making God 6
Song for the Moon Goddess 7
Green Man 8
    The Maiden Remains 9

Charges
Song of the Winter God 11
Grain God 12
The Horned God at
    Samhain 13
Old Yule God 14
Odinstave 15

Prayers / Turning the Wheel
Bird Call 17
Forgotten Gods 18
Beltane Joining 19
Solstice All Hail 20
Harvest 21
Samhain Chant 22

Blessings
Cup and Lady 24
God and Bread 25

Mystery Chants / Koans
The Path of Magic 27

Biographical / Experiential
Affirmation of a Pagan
    Priest 29
Credo for Tolerance and
    Understanding 30
Goddess Song 31
The Cradle 32
Shrine and Temple 33
Ritual 34
The Circle at Midnight 35
The Pentacle Man 36
The People of Ritual 37
Gathering 38
On the Heath 39

Invocations

Invocations are the special prayers, chants, and blessings used to open a Pagan or Wiccan (among other faiths) circle or ceremony. They prepare the sacred space and are used to facilitate aspecting, the Drawing Down of Goddess or God, to speak through the Priestess or Priest. They should always be spoken with the utmost reverence and respect.

A Circle Song

We are in this Place,
And this Place is in us, too.

We are in the Light,
And the Light is in us, too.

We are in the Dark,
And the Dark is in us, too.

We are in the Goddess,
The Lady, she is in us, too.

We are in the God,
Horned Lord, he is in us, too.

We are in the East,
And the Air is in us, too.

We are in the South,
And the Fire is in us, too.

We are in the West,
And the Water in us, too.

We are in the North,
And the Earth is in us, too.

We are in the Center,
And the Spirit in us, too.

We shall Circle round,
And the Circle surrounds us.

As we walk this Path,
This Path walks through Us.

Elemental Chant

Lord and Lady grant to me,
If it be Your Will,
These graces from Your Guardians,
Who We do call the Elements.

My breath as Air,
My Will as Fire,
My blood as Water,
My bones as Stone,
And my life as a Mirror,
To see Spirit.

Lord and Lady grant to me,
If it be Your Will,
These graces from Your Guardians,
Who We do call the Elements.

Let me breathe the quiet breath,
Let my will be unquenchable in Your service.
Quench my thirst with life and family,
Ground me on the Earth my Mother,
And Center me in Spirit.

Lord and Lady grant to me,
If it be Your Will,
These graces from Your Guardians,
Who We do call the Elements.

The Horned Lord at High Spring

Out of Winter,
Reborn with the world,
From the Earth His Mother,
Is the Glorious God,
Proof and Promise,
Of Our Renewal.

The Sun shines within Him,
And it is through His life,
That Flesh grows young and strong.
It is the Fire within his Blood,
That aids all men,
To see the Maiden.

His are the horns of lightning,
His fists the stone gray storm.
These are the twin hammers,
By grace of the Lady,
With which He smashes Winter,
On the Anvil of new life.

He is the Phoenix out of ashes,
He is Phoebus, the Brilliant,
Sword of the Waxing Year.
May Goddess grant,
Be it in flesh or leather,
He is always sheathed with Wisdom.

Out of Winter,
Reborn with the world,
From the Earth His Mother,
Is the Glorious God,
Proof and Promise,
Of Our Renewal.

Summer Lord

Horus and Apollo,
The God of Light and Day,
The Lord of High Summer,
Who walks the Shining Way.

His golden armour gleams,
With inner flames concealed,
To warm and warn the Earth,
Of fires best not revealed.

He is Lord of the Land,
Red King in the Blue Sky,
Our grain grows tall and strong,
Beneath His watchful Eye.

Rejoice in the Warm Time,
And even in the Burn,
As Cold comes soon enough,
For still the Wheel must Turn.

So praise the Hawk of Noon,
Or the Lyre of the Day,
For His Path leads to us,
But then must lead away.

But weep not forever,
He walks a well grooved Track,
The Path that leads Him off,
Will always bring Him back.

Horus and Apollo,
The God of Light and Day,
The Lord of High Summer,
Who Walks the Shining Way.

Sing the Making God

If yon man would be a Maker,
Chain fire to the Wheel,
Then he must bow to Lord Hephaestus,
And hammer to His Will.

If men would forge as dwarves do,
And dance the Anvil sound,
Then they must bow to noble Vulcan,
And centre to the ground.

If you trade in making,
Be it metal, glass, or clay,
Then you must sing to mighty Weyland,
When you work within His Way.

Every man has Work to do,
And every woman Called,
But if you would be a Maker,
You must Sing the Making God.

Song for the Moon Goddess

Silver Eye that scryes the ocean,
Shining Goddess, Queen of night,
Grant to Thy servants our petition,
Bless our journeys with Thy Light.

Great Lady who moves the waters,
Give us music when our hearts are still,
If we watch You with devotion,
Allow us to discern Your Will.

Each of us journeys in the darkness,
But we know that we are not alone,
For it is Your Hope we have to guide us,
And it is Your Face that will lead us home.

Green Man

God in the wood,
God of the wood,
God made of wood,
Grown in Green wood.

A Forest is,
A Cathedral,
A Green Man Wind,
Is a Mistral.

Green grow the Trees,
Round grows the Ring,
That marks the Hill,
Of the Green King.

An antlered Crown,
A Crown of Thorns,
A Hooded Man,
The Wild Horn.

The Sacred Woods,
Are Forest born,
Elder and Ash,
Oak and Hawthorn.

God in the wood,
God of the wood,
God made of wood,
Grown in Green wood.

The Maiden Remains (The Goddess at Imbolc)

Her hair is full of silver,
Bound and loosed by her own hand,
But her face is full of laughter,
And her soul its own command.

Tho the Lady be touched by Winter,
Her Heart knows Spring's refrain,
And were the bloom to wait one hundred turns,
Still the Maiden will Remain.

Three faces has the Goddess,
She cycles with the Land,
But in Her eyes the flowers live,
And will not meet the Wheel's demand.

Tho She walks one thousand times in darkness,
She is unfettered by Time's chain,
And whatever may wait at an eon's bequest,
Always will the Maiden Remain.

Charges

Charges are the term we generally apply to those utterances, prewritten or spontaneous, spoken by the Priest or Priestess while Aspecting, and speaking as the God or Goddess. Some of these are very famous and have been used within Wicca for over a half a century to the point that there is considerable dispute over the origin and authors' identities on some of these pieces. (All the ones here are by P. B. Owl.)

Song of the Winter God

The Mother has moved,
Left the lands of Harvest,
And with Her passing,
Has gone the Green.

They say She seeks,
The black wings say,
A son, a daughter,
A lover, a king.

What I know as truth,
Is that She is gone,
The land is cold,
The people in need.

Someone must hold,
The roof of the sky,
With bloodied spear,
And unblinking eye.

One alone must guard,
Land and children both,
Through cold and darkness,
Until the light returns.

Remember these words:

Love be not bound by Green,
Horns will guard the White,
And twixt Harvest and the Spring,
I will hold the Night.

Grain God

Gold Corn is My spear,
Brown Wheat is My stave,
To serve as a King,
I die like a Knave.

Mine is the Loaf Mass,
The breaking of bread,
I feed the living,
Sink roots in the dead.

The Sun is yet strong,
But sharp is the knife,
To feed the children,
I must give My life.

Eat of the Harvest,
But keep you My seed,
And I will rise up,
And answer your need.

I grow again green,
Must die in My gold,
For sacrifice means,
I never grow old.

Gold Corn is My spear,
Brown Wheat is My stave,
To serve as a King,
I die like a Knave.

The Horned God at Samhain

I am a thing of bark and wood,
I am made of antler and bone,
Mine is the footstep never heard,
You hear Me best walking alone.

I wear my scars as honour marks,
Gained in a long year of youth,
For I am He who guards the gate,
And serve both Goddess and Truth.

Mine are the ways hidden and hard,
And Mine are the roads through all Veils,
I am the holder of secrets,
But also a teller of Tales.

For when the Mother is barren,
And when the sky is storm cloud grey,
It is I who shield the children,
For dark winter night is my day.

So see My face in bark and wood,
Carve My fetish from old white bone,
When you hear steps that make no sounds,
Think of Me when you walk alone.

Old Yule God

When once I was young,
The Mother was green,
But now we are gray,
With what we have seen.

And in younger Time,
When I made the Light,
I gave the Earth warmth,
And made the day bright.

But now I am old,
With just one more task,
To bring the new Light,
In which She will bask.

For I bring not toys,
Nor sweets or yet coal,
I bring He who comes,
To warm the cold soul.

For as old light fades,
And must die by morn,
So the new enters,
And a young God born.

So weep for me not,
And stifle your cries,
If you still seek Me,
Just look in His Eyes.

And in younger Time,
When Heart is new bright,
I will come again,
And I will make Light.

Odinstave

I hurled my eye into the Dark,
Half Blinded to Self and by Self,
So that I in timeless time,
Could begin at last to See.

My Eye returned an Orb of Flame,
The Sun, the Moon, the Stars and Sea,
Black winged messengers to and fro,
These are My Thought and Memory.

I reached My hand into the void,
While bound and blinded on the Tree,
And then in My grasp did fall,
The Runes, the Glyphs, the Words to be.

I am Maker, Shaker, Oath Taker,
Wanderer, Wonderer, Wizardly,
Dreamer, Stave Carver, Riever,
King and Knave of Prophecy.

I hurled my eye into the Dark,
Half Blinded to Self and by Self,
So that I in timeless time,
Could begin at last to See.

Prayers/ Turning of the Wheel

Some prayers are just that, a call to the Divine either in request or in gratitude. In Wicca, and in other forms of Paganism, there is a form of prayer even simpler, where we "turn the wheel" and acknowledge the change in days or seasons and our connection to these changes.

Bird Call

Powers of the Sky,
If it be your will,
Grant me

The Strength of Eagle,
The Humility of Sparrow,
And the Song of Swallow.

Powers of the Sky,
If it be your will,
Grant me

The Laughter of Mockingbird,
The Passion of Robin,
And the Endurance of Pigeon.

Powers of the Sky,
If it be your will,
Grant me

The Wisdom of Owl,
The Mystery of Raven,
And the Hope of Phoenix.

Previously published in 13 Moons #3, Nov. 1998.

Forgotten Gods

All Gods Forgotten, Faded, Unknown,
Except in my dreams,
Where Your Glory is shown,
I ask Thy Blessings.

I ask Thy Blessings,
God of the Lost Places.
I ask Thy Blessings,
Goddess of Small Spaces.

I seek your Vision,
In a whisper, in a sigh.
I seek to see You,
In the corner of my eye.

Oh Thou scattered,
And scoured from the lands,
Excepting the way one man folds his hands,
I ask Thy Blessings.

All Gods Forgotten, Faded, Unknown,
Except in my dreams,
Where Your Glory is shown,
I ask Thy Blessings.

Beltane Joining

Our Goddess and Lord,
Green Earth and blue Sky,
Lay down together,
As do you and I.

Lord and Lady touch,
In perfect love and trust,
Make the strongest magic,
And it is the same for us.

All forms and all forces,
And so all fates and feys,
Must move with another,
And thus towards all grace.

All proceeds from love,
Which lies beneath us all,
As we sow in Springtime,
And harvest in the Fall.

Our Goddess and Lord,
Green Earth and blue Sky,
Will always lay together,
At times as you and I.

Solstice All Hail

Hail to the Sun
To Raise the Grain
To Reap and Sow
And Reap Again.

Hail to the Sun
To Light of Day
That Stands a Shield
Lest Night Hold Sway

Hail to the Sun
That Lights the Moon
To Give Shadows
The Glow of Noon

Hail to the Sun
For Lady, Lord
God to Goddess
And Truth to Word

Hail to the Sun
To Raise the Grain
To Reap and Sow
And Reap Again

Harvest

The year is ripe,
As is the grain,
And where we plant,
We reap again.

All fruit must fall,
And so all men,
Wonder not If,
Only ask When.

Plants will wither,
The land grow cold,
All Life harder,
And all men old.

But Harvest shows,
That all may grow,
And leave blessings,
In how they go.
And if our lives,
Must face the blade,
If others live,
A trade is made.

And if the freeze,
Must follow Fall,
Then view the scene,
And hear the Call.

For Goddess field,
And our Lord wheat,
Surround all things,
And are Complete.

If all must fall,
Both fruit and men,
When blossom comes,
We live again.

Harvest the grain,
Walk the old ways,
See the new life,
Give Them your praise.

For Time grows ripe,
Just like the grain,
And where we fall,
We grow again.

So from Harvest,
We are twice blessed,
In Spring new life,
In Autumn rest.

As fruit comes back,
So must all men,
Wonder not If,
Ask only When.

A Samhain Chant

Horned Lord hear us,
Stag behind the branch,
Guard the Lady Earth,
Ward her with Your lance.

She doth now grow old,
Harvest is now past,
Bow meat we ask for,
Lest our children fast.

Let our aim be true,
Winter need you see,
And in sight please grant,
Game beneath the tree.

The land is hard Lord,
We can no fruit seek,
We ask Thy blessing,
To cull Thy Herd's weak.

And when fruit ripens,
If we walk your lands,
And see spotted fawns,
We will stay our hands.

So Lord guide our aim,
In hand and in heart,
And teach us wisdom,
Speak the hunting art.

Horned Lord hear us,
Stag behind the branch,
Guard the Lady Earth,
Ward her with Your lance.

Blessings

Blessings are the special forms of prayers we use to consecrate and make holy. Most commonly these are the blessings on the sacred cup and cake during formal ritual (similar in some ways to Christian Communion) or the prayer before meals.

Cup and Lady

Lady and Cup,
All Fruit and Vine,
That which Nurtures,
Is Yours Divine.

Isis and Demeter,
Lady Most Great,
Golden Goddess,
Blue and Black Grapes.

Your Cauldron Births us,
As Wine from the Glass,
Your Earth Receives Us,
When Our Time has Passed.

When We Lift Sacred Cup,
And Drink from Holy Wine,
We save the sip for You,
For we Know we are Thine.

Lady and Cup,
All Fruit and Vine,
That which Nurtures,
Is Yours Divine.

Presented to the Moon's Inkwell Tradition of Wicca for liturgical use as a Cup Blessing, with publication rights for this usage to be retained by the Tradition in Perpetuity. All other publication rights to be retained by the author.

God and Bread

God and Bread,
Corn and Lord,
Life and Death,
Grain and Word.

Osiris and Attis,
King and Slain,
Bleeding God,
Growing Grain.

Honour feeds us,
From Sacrificed King,
Grain is the Mercy,
For which we Sing.

As you break the Bread,
Torn from Sacred Field,
Remember both Meanings,
The Lord Gives for Yield.

God and Bread,
Corn and Lord,
Life and Death,
Grain and Word.

Previously published in PagaNet News, Lammas 2004. Presented to the Moon's Inkwell Tradition of Wicca for liturgical use and Cake Blessing, with publication rights for this usage to be retained by the Tradition in perpetuity. All other publication rights to be retained by the author.

Mystery Chants/Koans:

A mystery chant or koan is designed to deepen our understanding of the Mysteries. Chants are normally meant to be repeated multiple times to let the energy of the mystery emerge from the words. In Wicca or Paganism the number of repetitions is normally a magically significant number such as 3, 5, 7, 9, 11, 13, or 21. Koans (the term is from Zen practice) are stories that hopefully point the way towards enlightenment. Here is an example.

The Path of Magic (Mantra of the Initiate)

The Mage traces the lines of the shattered Symbolon
The Wizard sends these lines as Holy Fire from his fingers
The Shaman uses Holy Fire to Heal the Wounded Man
The Healed Man knows in Truth that God is Ever present.

God from Healing speaks and then there is the Word
The Word self scribes on the face of the Symbolon
The Mystic shatters the Symbolon into Myriad
Lest it cast a shadow to obscure the Face of God.

The Mage traces the lines of the shattered Symbolon
The Wizard sends these lines as Holy Fire from his fingers
The Shaman uses Holy Fire to Heal the Wounded Man
The Healed Man knows in Truth that God is Ever present.

God from Healing speaks and then there is the Word
The Word self scribes on the face of the Symbolon
The Mystic shatters the Symbolon into Myriad
Lest it cast a shadow to obscure the Face of God.

The Mage traces the lines of the shattered Symbolon
The Wizard sends these lines as Holy Fire from his fingers
The Shaman uses Holy Fire to Heal the Wounded Man
The Healed Man knows in Truth that God is Ever present.

God from Healing speaks and then there is the Word
The Word self scribes on the face of the Symbolon
The Mystic shatters the Symbolon into Myriad
Lest it cast a shadow to obscure the Face of God.

Biographical/Experiental

These poems are about experiences, mine and those of my community. In some ways these are the most personal.

Affirmation of a Pagan Priest

I am who I am,
I am no other,
I am not my Father,
I am not my Mother.
I am who I am,
I will be no other.

I am who I am,
I am no other,
I will honour the Earth,
For I am her Brother.
I am who I am,
I will be no other.

I am who I am,
I am no other,
And he who I am,
I shall strive to discover,
I am who I am,
I will be no other.

Credo for Tolerance and Understanding

We have faith.
It is not your faith.
We have hope.
It is not your hope.
We have dreams.
They are not your dreams.

You ask what we are,
And we say to you:

We are faithful.
We are hopeful.
And we seek the vision.
Just as you are.
And just as you do.

Goddess Song

We are those,
Who Love a Goddess,
We are those,
Who bless Her name.

We are children,
Of the Mystery,
Guardians, Keepers,
Of Her Flame.

If you walk,
The glade at Midnight,
You will see,
Our Goddess there.

If not in Her form.
Then in ours,
Our Souls, Her Eyes,
Our Lives, Her Hair.

Walk the forest,
If only once,
Bare your life,
On a starry plain.

Find your way here,
Once unguided,
To gain Her guidance,
Forever and again.

The Cradle

Our cradle was a River,
In the Land as Black as Night,
Our faith and dreams, all hopes as well,
Were born in the Desert of Light.

Here dwelled Aset, the Queen,
The Goddess Red and Blue,
Greatest Mother, She Who Searched,
Men call Her Isis, too.

Here was Horus, Hawk of Day,
Swift God of Sky and Flight,
Containing Ra, His elder Self,
We are safe in Heru's Sight.

Each full Circle of the Wheel,
Saw the River wash the Land,
Bringing Grain, and Life's renewal,
To the Shapings of Ptah's Hand.

I have left the Cradle,
And the Land has greyed in hue,
But Still I praise Tehuti,
Ibis Thoth who wrote words true.

Our Cradle was a River,
In a Land as Black as Night,
Our Faith, Our Dreams, Our Hopes still Dwell,
From Their Birth in the Desert of Light.

Shrine and Temple

Shrine and temple,
Field and fen,
Sacred spaces,
That we ken.

Here the tree,
Here the well,
Here the ring,
Where fey folk dwell.

Here the barrow,
Filled with gold,
Here the hero,
In legend told.

Standing stones,
The village green,
Power felt,
Not often seen.

Cave of wisdom,
Hidden spring,
By the shore,
Where rests the king.

At the temple,
In the shrine,
We are seekers,
Of Divine.

Ritual

We circle and we sing,
We dance the spiral round,
We ask the Gods for wisdom,
And Call the power down.

We consecrate with Salt,
Are blessed by Fire and Air,
The Lady's Tears are Water,
Her face reflected there.

We Work within the Circle,
Outside of Time and Space,
We gather in the Night,
To feel the Lady's Grace.

The Lord of Hunts we know,
Of old he is our guide,
We hear within our hearts,
The hoof beats of His Ride.

We are the Circling Ones,
We ask for joy, not gain,
We dance for all who ask,
For balm against the pain.

We circle and we sing,
We feel the ebb and flow,
And when the Gods do will,
We let the power go.

We circle and we sing,
We dance the spiral round,
We ask the Gods for wisdom,
And call the Power down.

The Circle at Midnight

While others sleep and dream,
We are Dreamers and awake,
The dreams they seek in sleep,
It is our hope to make.

Ours the circle in the stars,
And ours the midnight sun,
In the deep of middle night,
We see the work is done.

For some must guard the vale,
And hold the wolves at bay,
Some must walk the sword bridge,
And hold until the day.

And if our way is dark,
Think not we shun the light,
We are shadows walking,
To keep the morning bright.

You who sleep and dream,
Dream of Dreamers awake,
Your dream of light and hope,
Our vigil was to make.

The Pentacle Man

I wear a Symbol at my breast,
A Sign of Rede and Path,
It has been met with Hate and Fear,
(Sometimes you have to laugh).

For as Old Leonardo drew,
And as Star in Circle doth reveal,
As a Man, I am a Star,
And at all points, I touch the Wheel.

The People of Ritual

We stand in Sacred Space,
And it is our standing,
That makes the space so sacred.

We are the Heart of the Goddess,
And the Hands of the Horned Lord,
We are the Lifeblood of Creation,
Feel our flow.

We are the People of the Work,
And where there is a break,
We strive for mending,
And weave the web of Community.

You stand in Sacred Space,
And it is your understanding,
That makes the space so sacred.

Blessed Be.

Previously published in 13 Moons #5, Imbolc (Feb.) 1999.

Gathering

Lone and quiet as we may live,
It is together we are called.
In the fey festivals of the far places,
We sing our praises to the gods.

In field or in forest,
Our flags are unfurled,
Here we build the hidden city,
That dares to shape the world.

From every walk of life,
From every trade we come,
Our hands we bring to serve,
Our hearts to make the drum.

We serve the hidden ways,
We wear the face of Man,
We keep the Magic in our hearts,
And reveal it when we can.

Lone and quiet as you may live,
It is together you are called,
Join the fey festivals of the far places,
And sing your praises to the gods.

On the Heath

I walk the path unknown,
Terra Incognita, the Unmarked Way.
Far from firmer roads,
Stamped solid by many feet.

From this path of mine,
I have seen the Faery ride,
Viewed Fire in the hills,
And heard the speech of Stars.

Lao Tzu once walked,
On ground nearby,
In thought and heart,
If not in longitude.

Tho the shape of my foot
Be made by Catholics and Calvinists,
I dwell in the Far Country,
And my steps are on the Heath.

About the Author

P. B. Owl holds a 3rd Degree through the WynDragon Tradition of Wicca, and also serves as an Elder in this Tradition and in the Moon's Inkwell and CeltiaDraconis Traditions of Wicca. Since 1995, his articles (as P. B. Owl) and poetry (as Burrowing Owl) have appeared in "Paganet News", "13 Moons", "Waxing and Waning", "Fagan", "WynterGreen", "The Starlight Gathering", "GreenEggzine" and THE PAGAN'S MUSE (ed Jane Raeburn, Citadel Press).

He is a founding member of the WynDragon Family, an East TN based Wiccan seminary founded in 1999, where he serves as Man in Black.

This is his first book.

www.ingramcontent.com/pod-product-compliance
Lightning Source LLC
Chambersburg PA
CBHW072041060426
42449CB00010BA/2387